All Families

Multiracial Families

by Connor Stratton

FOCUS READERS

BEACON

www.focusreaders.com

Focus Readers is distributed by North Star Editions:
sales@northstareditions.com | 888-417-0195

Produced for Focus Readers by Red Line Editorial.

Photographs ©: iStockphoto, cover, 1; Shutterstock Images, 4, 6, 8, 11, 12, 14–15, 16, 19, 21, 22, 24, 26, 29

Library of Congress Cataloging-in-Publication Data
Names: Stratton, Connor, author.
Title: Multiracial families / by Connor Stratton.
Description: Mendota Heights, MN: Focus Readers, [2025] | Series: All families | Includes bibliographical references and index. | Audience: Grades 2-3
Identifiers: LCCN 2024034094 (print) | LCCN 2024034095 (ebook) | ISBN 9798889983934 (hardcover) | ISBN 9798889984214 (paperback) | ISBN 9798889984764 (pdf) | ISBN 9798889984498 (ebook)
Subjects: LCSH: Racially mixed families--Juvenile literature.
Classification: LCC HQ1031 .S8253 2025 (print) | LCC HQ1031 (ebook) | DDC 306.850973--dc23/eng/20240820
LC record available at https://lccn.loc.gov/2024034094
LC ebook record available at https://lccn.loc.gov/2024034095

Printed in the United States of America
Mankato, MN
012025

About the Author

Connor Stratton writes and edits nonfiction children's books. He lives in Minnesota.

Table of Contents

HOLD IT
REFILL IT
ProVision
ATD
STOP
Notice of Additional Screening
Carry on bags waiting for additional screening
DO NOT REMOVE
STOP

Chapter 1

Visiting Family Overseas

A girl and her parents are going through airport security. A worker looks at the girl. Then he looks at her parents. He asks the girl lots of questions. He isn't sure if they are all one family.

For many people, going through airport security can be stressful.

Spending time with family helps people stay connected to one another.

The girl is confused. She feels mad, too. Is it because she looks different? The girl's skin is light brown. Her dad has dark brown skin. And her mom's skin is light like peach.

Finally, the family gets through. They fly to another country. Her dad's whole family greets them. The girl gets lots of big hugs. She speaks her dad's language. She's so glad to be with her big family again.

People in the United States speak more than 350 languages.

Chapter 2

About Multiracial Families

Race is a way of putting people into different groups. Race is mostly based on how people look. Skin color is one main way people are grouped. Other **physical** features can matter, too.

People can have a wide variety of skin colors, hair textures, and other features.

Race is also connected to **ethnicity**. It can be tied to **culture** as well.

Humans invented race. It is not found in nature. It is not rooted in science. Society values some races more than others. It tends to put white people at the top. People of color are often treated unfairly. This unfair treatment is called racism.

Even so, many people oppose racism. And they take pride in who they are. They celebrate how they look. They explore their culture.

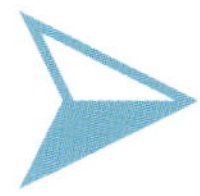

Black people are more likely than white people to be stopped by police. That is one example of racism.

They respect other people's backgrounds, too.

In some families, members have different races. These are called multiracial families. They may also be known as mixed-race families.

In the United States, more than 33 million people are multiracial.

For example, one parent might be Black. The other parent might be Asian. Their children may **identify** as just one of these races. Or they may see themselves as both Black and Asian. The way people identify can also change over time.

In addition, one parent may be multiracial. Or both parents might be. **Blended families** can also be mixed-race. There are many kinds of multiracial families.

By the early 2020s, about 10 percent of people in the United States were multiracial.

MANY IDENTITIES

Blended Families

Some multiracial families are blended. Stepsiblings may have different skin colors. That can put children in tough situations. Strangers may treat stepsiblings differently. They might be kind to a light-skinned sibling. But they might be mean to a sibling with darker skin.

If this happens, it can feel painful. It can also be confusing. Talking about what happened can help. Stepsiblings can also embrace their differences. Siblings who look different are as much a family as any other.

About 3 of every 20 kids in the United States live in blended families.

Chapter 3

Challenges

Being part of a multiracial family can have challenges. Multiracial kids may be treated poorly. For example, some people believe **stereotypes** about certain groups. Many stereotypes are about race.

In the early 2020s, most multiracial people were under the age of 18.

Sometimes people repeat those stereotypes. Hearing them can feel hurtful.

Mixed-raced people also face confusion from others. People might ask, "What are you?" Or they may say, "You don't look like your

Multiracial children might feel they have to choose one of their identities. However, they know that's just one part of who they are.

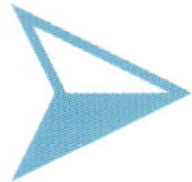

It's normal to feel upset when classmates make rude comments.

parents." That can put multiracial kids in a tough spot. They may feel that they have to defend part of themselves.

Visits with **extended family** can also be hard for multiracial kids.

For example, one side of the family might be white. The lighter-skinned cousins may be treated differently. Then, suppose the other side of the family speaks a different language. Kids may feel left out as a result. Sometimes, multiracial children feel like they don't fit in anywhere. That can feel lonely.

Many multiracial kids don't have multiracial parents. Parents always try to understand their kids. But they may not fully understand what

Visits with grandparents can sometimes be challenging for multiracial kids.

it's like. Also, some families try to avoid talking about race. It can be a difficult topic. However, it's important to **communicate**.

Chapter 4

Dealing with Challenges

Mixed-race kids are not always understood. In response, kids may have many emotions. They might feel angry. They might feel sad. Confusion can come up. Some kids may feel all these things.

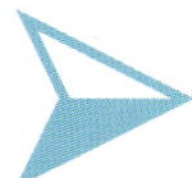

People may have big feelings when they don't feel understood.

Talking to a counselor can help some kids express their feelings.

Kids might also feel like they have to fit in. So, they may pretend not to care.

All of these responses make sense. And they are all okay. Still, expressing feelings is important. Kids can talk to trusted adults. Writing about it can help, too.

Other people who share the same race can help, too. This might be an extended family member. Or it could be new friends. That way, kids can connect to their cultures.

Children may also want to find other mixed-race kids. The other kids might not share the same racial background. But they know what it's like to be multiracial.

Love is what makes a family, not skin color.

Being part of a multiracial family is a strength, too. From a young age, kids learn that everyone is different. They experience more than one culture. They gain an understanding of what different groups go through.

Children in multiracial families are perfect as they are. They can be who they want to be. And they can call themselves what they want. It's okay if they don't look like other family members. That's still their family.

Experiencing different cultures can teach **empathy**.

FOCUS ON

Multiracial Families

Write your answers on a separate piece of paper.

1. Summarize the main ideas of Chapter 4.
2. What are some differences within your family?
3. In the early 2020s, what percent of people in the United States were multiracial?
    - A. less than 1 percent
    - B. about 10 percent
    - C. more than 70 percent
4. How can experiencing different cultures teach people empathy?
    - A. They learn that all cultures are the same.
    - B. They learn that their way of communicating is the only way.
    - C. They learn about more ways other people feel and communicate.

5. What does **emotions** mean in this book?

*Mixed-race kids are not always understood. In response, kids may have many **emotions**. They might feel angry. They might feel sad. Confusion can come up.*

A. feelings
B. answers
C. ages

6. What does **expressing** mean in this book?

*Still, **expressing** feelings is important. Kids can talk to trusted adults. Writing about it can help, too.*

A. feeling something painful
B. putting something into words
C. listening to something closely

Answer key on page 32.

Glossary

blended families
Families that include children from earlier relationships.

communicate
To make something known to others.

culture
A group of people and how they live, such as customs and beliefs.

empathy
The ability to understand the feelings of other people.

ethnicity
National or cultural qualities that connect a group of people.

extended family
Family members outside of parents and siblings. They can include grandparents, aunts, uncles, cousins, and more.

identify
To say what someone is.

physical
Having to do with the body.

stereotypes
Oversimplified, unfair, or untrue ideas about what all members of a certain group are like.

To Learn More

BOOKS

Johnson, Chelsea, LaToya Council, and Carolyn Choi. *Love Without Bounds: An IntersectionAllies Book About Families*. New York: Dottir Press, 2023.

McClain, AnneMarie, and Lacey Hilliard. *Talking About Racism*. Ann Arbor, MI: Cherry Lake Publishing, 2023.

Uhl, Xina M. *Acceptance, Respect, and Appreciation of Difference*. Buffalo, NY: PowerKids Press, 2023.

NOTE TO EDUCATORS

Visit **www.focusreaders.com** to find lesson plans, activities, links, and other resources related to this title.

Index

Answer Key: 1. Answers will vary; **2.** Answers will vary; **3.** B; **4.** C; **5.** A; **6.** B